rockschool®

Piano

US Level 1 (UK Grade 1)

Performance pieces, technical exercises, supporting tests and in-depth guidance for Rockschool assessments

All accompanying and supporting audio can be downloaded from: *www.rslawards.com/downloads*

Input the following code when prompted: **5LPRSEJN26**

For more information, turn to page 5

Acknowledgements

Published by Rockschool Ltd. © 2019 & 2020
Catalogue Number: RSK200090US
ISBN: 978-1-78936-166-7
Initial US Release | Errata details can be found at *www.rslawards.com/errata*

SYLLABUS
Syllabus designed and written by Jono Harrison
Syllabus Director: Tim Bennett-Hart
Syllabus consultants: Gary Sanctuary, Chris Stanbury, Simon Troup and Jennie Troup
Hit Tune arrangements by Jono Harrison and Gary Sanctuary
Supporting Tests written by Jono Harrison, Chris Stanbury, Nik Preston and Ash Preston
Syllabus advisors: Tim Bennett-Hart, Brian Ashworth, Stuart Slater, Peter Huntington, Bruce Darlington, Simon Troup and Jennie Troup

PUBLISHING
Proof reading of arrangements by Sharon Kelly, Simon Troup, Jennie Troup and Jono Harrison
Music engraving and book layout by Simon and Jennie Troup of Digital Music Art
Fact files written and edited by Abbie Thomas
Notes written by Roland Perrin
Proof reading and copy editing by Gemma Bull, Jono Harrison and Jennie Troup
Cover design by Philip Millard of Rather Nice Design
Cover photograph: © Nomad_Soul (Shutterstock)

AUDIO
Produced by Jono Harrison
Engineered by Jono Harrison, Gary Sanctuary, Tim Bennett-Hart, Pete Riley, Richard Brook, Rory Harvey and Andy Robertson
Assisted by Paul Pritchard at Abbey Road
Recorded at Dock Street Studios, The Dairy and Abbey Road
Mixed by Patrick Phillips
Mastered by Francis Gorini

Supporting Tests recorded by Chris Stanbury and Jono Harrison

MUSICIANS
Piano and Keyboards: Jono Harrison, Gary Sanctuary, Ross Stanley & Tania Ilyashova
Drums & Percussion: Pete Riley and Richard Brook
Bass & Synth Bass: Andy Robertson
Guitars: Rory Harvey, Nat Martin and Jono Harrison
Saxophone: Jonathan Griffiths
Trombone: Tom George White and Norton York
Trumpet: Nick Mead and John Simpson
Lead and Backing Vocals: Glen Harvey & Katie Hector
Additional Programming: Jono Harrison

DISTRIBUTION
Exclusive Distributors: Hal Leonard

CONTACTING ROCKSCHOOL
www.rslawards.com
Telephone: +44 (0)345 460 4747
Email: *info@rslawards.com*

EXECUTIVE PRODUCERS
John Simpson, Norton York

Awarding the Contemporary Arts

Table of Contents

Welcome to Rockschool Piano Level/Grade 1

Welcome to Rockschool's Piano syllabus 2019. This syllabus is designed to support pianists in their progression from Debut to Level/Grade 8, through an engaging and rigorous pathway covering all the genres, stylistic elements, techniques and musical skills required for success as a contemporary pianist.

Piano Assessments
At each level/grade you have the option of taking one of two different types of assessment:

- Level/**Grade Assessment**
  A Level/Grade Assessment is a mixture of music performances, technical work and tests. You are required to prepare three pieces (two of which may be Free Choice Pieces) and the contents of the Technical Exercise section. This accounts for 75% of the assessment marks. The other 25% consists of: either a Sight Reading or an Improvisation & Interpretation test (10%), two Ear Tests (10%), and finally you will be asked five General Musicianship Questions (5%). The pass mark is 60%.

- **Performance Certificate**
  A Performance Certificate is equivalent to a Level/Grade Assessment, but in a Performance Certificate you are required to perform five pieces. A maximum of three of these can be Free Choice Pieces. Each song is marked out of 20 and the pass mark is 60%.

All elements required to participate in a Rockschool assessment can be found in the level/grade book. These are as follows:

- **Assessment Pieces**
  The 2019 syllabus comprises six 'hit tune' arrangements, benchmarked and devised so as to equip contemporary pianists with industry-relevant skills in any performance environment. These fall into three categories:

  Melody & Accompaniment
  These arrangements are performed to full band backing tracks, with the piano performing both melody and accompaniment

  Solo Piano Arrangement
  These are full solo piano arrangements, performed without backing tracks

  Vocal Accompaniment
  These arrangements cover the skills required of contemporary pianists in ensemble environments, be they on the stage or in the studio. The backing tracks feature vocalists, and the piano parts are reflective of what session pianists would perform live or on mainstream commercial recordings

  Each 'hit tune' arrangement is preceded by a Fact File, giving surrounding context to the piece and the original performers/recording artists.

  Furthermore, at the end of each arrangement you will find notes giving additional supportive context to get the most out of the pieces.

- **Technical Exercises**
  There are either three or four groups of technical exercise, depending on the level/grade:

  Debut–Level/Grade 8:
  Group A: Scales
  Group B: Arpeggios/Broken Chords
  Group C: Chord Voicings

  Levels/Grades 4–8 only:
  Group D: Technical Study

- **Supporting Tests**
  There are three types of unprepared supporting tests in the assessment:

  1. The first type can be one of two options (this is the *candidate's* choice):

     Either:
     Sight Reading tests, developing the musician's ability to read and perform previously unseen material;

     or:
     Improvisation & Interpretation tests, developing the musician's ability to develop previously unseen material in a stylistic way and perform improvised passages of melody. The book contains examples of both types of test – equivalent 'unseen' examples will be provided for the assessment

  2. **Ear Tests**
     Debut–Level/Grade 3: feature Melodic Recall and Chord Recognition
     Levels/Grades 4–8: feature Melodic Recall and Harmonic Recall

  3. **General Musicianship Questions (GMQs)**, which you will be asked by the assessor at the end of each assessment

General Information

You will find information on assessment procedures, including online assessment entry, marking schemes, information on Free Choice Pieces and improvisation requirements for each level/grade.

Audio

In addition to the level/grade book, we have also provided audio in the form of backing tracks (minus piano) and full tracks (including piano) for all 'hit tune' arrangements, technical exercises and supporting tests (where applicable). We have provided professional performance recordings of all solo piano pieces in the syllabus. This audio can be downloaded from RSL directly at *www.rslawards.com/downloads*

You will need to input this code when prompted: **5LPRSEJN26**

The audio files are supplied in MP3 format. Once downloaded you will be able to play them on any compatible device.

Further Information

You can find further details about Rockschool's Contemporary Piano syllabus by downloading the syllabus guide from our website: *www.rslawards.com*

All candidates should download and read the accompanying syllabus guide when using this level/grade book.

Performance and Technical Guidance

Fingering
Any fingering annotation is given as a guide only.

Interpretation
Notation should be performed exactly as written, except where there are performance indications to ad. lib, improvise, develop, etc. In these instances, the candidate will be marked on their ability to interpret the music in a stylistically appropriate way, commensurate with the level.

Adaptation
A small degree of adaptation is allowed where, for example, hand stretches do not facilitate the required notated parts. Marks may be deducted if adaptation results in over-simplification of the notation. If in doubt you can submit any adaptation enquiries to *info@rslawards.com*

Articulation & Dynamics
Where articulation and dynamics are marked on the notation, they should be followed. Where it is open to interpretation, the candidate is free to take their own approach.

Pedalling
The candidate may use the pedal freely at any level/grade, but it should be applied judiciously as marks may be deducted for any over usage resulting in an unclear tone. In addition, where pedalling is written into (or out of) the notation, this should be observed.

Chord Symbols
Most hit tune arrangements have chord symbols written above the notation. This is purely for guidance, and to assist the candidate and teacher.

Tattooed Heart

SONG TITLE: 'TATTOOED HEART'
ALBUM: YOURS TRULY
RELEASED: 2013
LABEL: REPUBLIC
GENRE: POP/R&B
WRITTEN BY: GRANDE/BABYFACE/RIDDICK-TYNES/THOMAS III/DIXON/SQUIRE/SEAN FOREMAN
PRODUCED BY: BABYFACE/DIXON/THE RASCALS/SQUIRE/NATHANIEL MOTTE
US CHART PEAK: 31

'Tattooed Heart' is the fourth song to feature on Ariana Grande's debut studio album, *Yours Truly.* Although never released as a single, the song has over 7 million views on YouTube and over 44 million streams on Spotify. The album from which it stems was met by critical acclaim, with many reviewers being surprised by its sophistication and Grande's vocal capabilities. Many compared Grande to the likes on Mariah Carey, which doesn't surprise as she is renowned for her ability to mimic others.

Ariana Grande was born in Florida in 1993 to Italian heritage and began her showbusiness career at the young age of 15, starring in Broadway musical '13'. She then went on to fill the role of Cat Valentine for Nickelodeon's television series 'Victorious', with whom she launched her music career by featuring on the official *Music from Victorious* (2011) soundtrack. Her debut album, *Yours Truly,* was released in 2013 and topped the US Billboard album charts, whilst peaking at number 7 in the UK. Grande lists her influences for *Yours Truly* as Whitney Houston, Amy Winehouse, Christina Aguilera and Mariah Carey, detailing that much of the album is a homage to the R&B sounds of the 90s which many of these talented singers contributed to. The album also had top ten success in Australia, Canada, Denmark, The Netherlands, and Japan.

Grande has released four studio albums, all of which debuted in the top ten of the UK album charts, and has three UK number 1 singles so far. With her fifth studio album *Thank U, Next* due for release soon, it can only be assumed that her success will continue and she'll have yet another top ten album to be proud of. The lead single from the up and coming album of the same name recently broke a UK Chart record and now claims the highest number of streams in a week, hitting 14.9 million and overtaking Ed Sheeran's 'Shape of You' which previously held the record at 14.2 million.

Although she is yet to win a Grammy, Grande does have six nominations to her name and has won three American Music Awards, two NME awards and a long list of many more.

Tattooed Heart

Ariana Grande

Words & Music by Kenneth Edmonds, Antonio Dixon, Matthew Squire, Ariana Grande, Sean Foreman, Leon Thomas & Khristopher Van Riddick Tynes

Em
D
(8va)
[19]
C
C♯
(8va)
[21]
D
(8va)
[23]
C
G
D7/F♯
Em
[25]
D
C
C♯
[28]
D
G
[31]

Notes

Although there are no eighth-note rhythms in the piano part, teachers might think about preparing students for other songs by discussing the concept of swing feel – perhaps by explaining that swing feel skips, rather than ticking like a clock.

This song is influenced by pop music from the 1950's, and teachers might enjoy listening to Elvis Presley ('Can't Help Falling In Love') and The Righteous Brothers ('Unchained Melody') with students. Understanding the context and history of songs can help deepen the student's engagement with the music.

It is important that students should keep a steady pulse throughout Section A. In slow moving passages of music, the challenge lies in avoiding the temptation to pre-empt each chord and inadvertently speed up. Practise the right hand separately before adding in the left-hand bass line. When you put both hands together, make sure to listen carefully and aim for all notes within the chord to sound clearly and precisely at the same time.

Pay careful attention to the *staccato* chords in measures 8 and 16. Remember that *staccato* chords are different from accented chords. Aim to keep the volume the same as the previous measure and count the following rests carefully.

In measures 17 to 24, the left hand plays quite high in the treble clef. Students will need to learn to move their left arm across their body, and must be discouraged from moving to the right of the piano stool. Teacher must also ensure that students maintain a straight back during this passage.

Section C is a repeat of the opening first 8 measures of the piece. Be careful to observe the tied whole-note rhythm in measures 33 and 34, holding the chord right to the end of the final measure of the piece.

Hallelujah

SONG TITLE: 'HALLELUJAH'
ALBUM: GRACE
RELEASED: 2007
LABEL: COLUMBIA
GENRE: FOLK/ALTERNATIVE ROCK
WRITTEN BY: LEONARD COHEN
PRODUCED BY: JEFF BUCKLEY/ ANDY WALLACE
US CHART PEAK: 1 (2008)

This song was written and originally released by Canadian singer songwriter Leonard Cohen. Featuring on his 1984 album *Various Positions*, the track initially found little success and peaked at number 59 on the US Billboard singles chart. It is with Jeff Buckley's 1994 version that the song received the critical acclaim it deserved. Certainly a songwriter's masterpiece, Cohen delivered a powerful lyric and melody. However, it was Buckley's haunting vocal and arrangement that saw the song peak at number 2 in the UK Singles Chart.

Jeff Buckley featured his version of the track on his one and only album, *Grace (1994)*. Hallelujah was never officially released as a single at the time and featured only as an album track. It wasn't until ten years after Buckley's untimely passing that the song was released as a single in 2007. Since it's release, Buckley's version has been held as one of the greatest interpretations of all time and is regarded highly by artists to this day. John Legend famously reports that Buckley's posthumous release is '…one of the most beautiful pieces of recorded music I've ever heard.'

In 2004 'Rolling Stone Magazine' ranked Buckley's rendition at number 259 in their 'The 500 Greatest Songs of All Time' list, long before its single release. In 2007, Buckley's 'Hallelujah' was named 'The Greatest Song of All Time' by The International Observer. It seemed that at last the mastery of the song was receiving the acclaim it deserved.

Jeff Buckley's album *Grace* was released in 1994 and initially achieved poor sales, peaking at number 149 in the US Billboard Album Chart. However, by 2007 the album as a worldwide success and had sales of over 2 million copies globally. *Grace* has been cited by critics and listeners as one of the greatest albums of all time. Sadly, Jeff Buckley never lived to see the success of his work and will never know the impression his adaption of Hallelujah had on its listeners. At six and a half minutes long, his version takes the listener on a whirlwind of emotions, with constant highs and lows his vocal is mesmerising to listen to and the lyrics can be heard far clearer than on Cohen's original. Of course, the credit for writing such a beautiful piece remains Cohen's but had it not been for Buckley's interpretation we may never have known the genius of the lyric.

Hallelujah

Jeff Buckley

1.
F
Am
mp
[21]
F
C
G
[25]
C
Am
C
Am
p
[29]
2.
F
Am
F
mp
[33]
C
G
C
p
[38]

Notes

The tender, semi-religious feel of this song needs to be mirrored by the performer's careful following of the dynamic markings – the playing must never rise above the marked ***mf***.

The opening four measures help set the mood of the piece and should be played *legato*, allowing the flowing pattern to pass evenly between the hands.

After the simple introduction, the left hand takes on a more of an accompanying role while the right hand should be allowed to take the lead, continuing to play *legato*. Be careful not to allow this shift in roles to lead to an increase in the overall volume, and strive to maintain the gentle quiet mood established in the introduction.

Note that the lyrical melody line in the right-hand part starts on the final eighth-note of measure 4 and not at the start of measure 5! This is also the case for the final eighth note at the end of the first time repeat in measure 32.

It is worth spending time practicing the left hand part separately to secure all of your hand position changes when moving from one chord voicing to the next. Pay particular attention to the hand position change when moving from the G major chord position in measure 17 to the E major chord in measure 18. Playing these two measures in isolation at a slower tempo will help to secure a confident and quick change.

From measure 21 onwards, many measures contain longer, sustained rhythm patterns. It will be important to keep the pulse steady to avoid speeding up or slowing down.

Can You Feel The Love Tonight

SONG TITLE: 'CAN YOU FEEL THE LOVE TONIGHT'
ALBUM: THE LION KING: ORIGINAL MOTION PICTURE SOUNDTRACK
RELEASED: 1994
LABEL: WALT DISNEY
GENRE: POP
WRITTEN BY: ELTON JOHN/TIM RICE
PRODUCED BY: CHRIS THOMAS
US CHART PEAK: 4

'Can You Feel the Love Tonight' was written by Elton John and Tim Rice. The pair were commissioned to write the song for Disney's 1994 musical release of 'The Lion King', the 32nd animated feature film to be released by the conglomerate. John and Rice are well known for their partnership, with John on composition and rice on lyrics, and they did not disappoint. They tell a moving tale of responsibility and love, delivered perfectly by the cast for the in-scene film version; Kristle Edwards, Joseph Williams, Sally Dworsky, Nathan Lee and Ernie Sabella.

Elton John's recording of 'Can You Feel the Love Tonight' was released approximately six weeks before the film was due to hit the box office, working as promotion for Disney's latest release. This proved a successful marketing technique and John's recording made it to number 4 on the US Billboard Singles Chart and number 14 in the UK. With sales of over one million copies, the song was certified as Platinum in the US. On its release, 'The Lion King' took the box office by storm with an initial gross of $766 million and finished its theatrical run as the highest-grossing release of 1994.

Elton John was born Reginald Kenneth Dwight in 1947 and grew up in the Pinner area of London. He began playing the piano at a very young age and soon became interested in songwriting. He met his long-term writing partner, Bernie Taupin, in 1967 when they both responded to an advertisement seeking songwriters. Together the duo wrote hits for existing artists (such as Lulu) for two years, before John released his debut album in 1969. Since then, they have achieved unmeasurable success and have collaborated on more than 30 albums.

Elton John was appointed a CBE in 1995 and was knighted by Queen Elizabeth II in 1998 for his commendable charity work. He has been performing for more than five decades and has sold more than 300 million records worldwide, making him one of the best-selling music artists of all time. 'Can You Feel the Love Tonight' won John his first Academy Award in 1995 for 'Best Original Song', he actually had three nominations in that same category for that same year, all of which were compositions for 'The Lion King'. He has been nominated for 34 Grammy Awards, five of which he has won including the Grammy Legend Award in 2000. His songwriting has certainly been acknowledged as outstanding, with a staggering ten wins at the Ivor Novello Awards over the years.

Can You Feel The Love Tonight

Elton John

From 'The Lion King' (1994)

Music by Elton John
Lyrics by Tim Rice

1.
G C C♯m7♭5 D C G/D
[15]
Em7 G/D C Am G/B C C♯m7♭5 D
[18]
2.
C G/B Em7 G/D C Am G/B C6 Dsus4
[21]
Gsus4 G C G
p
[24]
Em7 D C Am G/B C6 Dsus4 Gsus4 G
[26]

Notes

This is a simple, romantic ballad and students should make sure they play the song at the correct tempo in order to be true to the sentiment of the lyrics.

As the left-hand part moves from a half-note rhythm pattern to quarter-notes from measure 4 onwards, it can be tempting for students to allow the tempo to speed up. To avoid this, students should have a clear quarter-note pulse in mind before beginning the piece.

Note that the rhythm pattern in the right-hand part of measure 5 is syncopated. Take time to work out clearly where each note falls between the two parts by slowing down the tempo and playing the measure in isolation until secure. Time would be well spent identifying where this pattern repeats and noting where it differs, for example in measure 7.

To improve the effectiveness of the song, students should be aware of the contrast in articulation between the right hand and the left hand. The right hand should maintain a smooth, singing *legato*, whilst the left hand should add impetus by allowing a small amount of separation when playing the quarter notes.

Wildest Dreams

SONG TITLE: 'WILDEST DREAMS'
ALBUM: 1989
RELEASED: 2014
LABEL: BIG MACHINE/REPUBLIC
GENRE: DREAM POP
WRITTEN BY: TAYLOR SWIFT/ MAX MARTIN/SHELLBACK
PRODUCED BY: MAX MARTIN/SHELLBACK
US CHART PEAK: 5

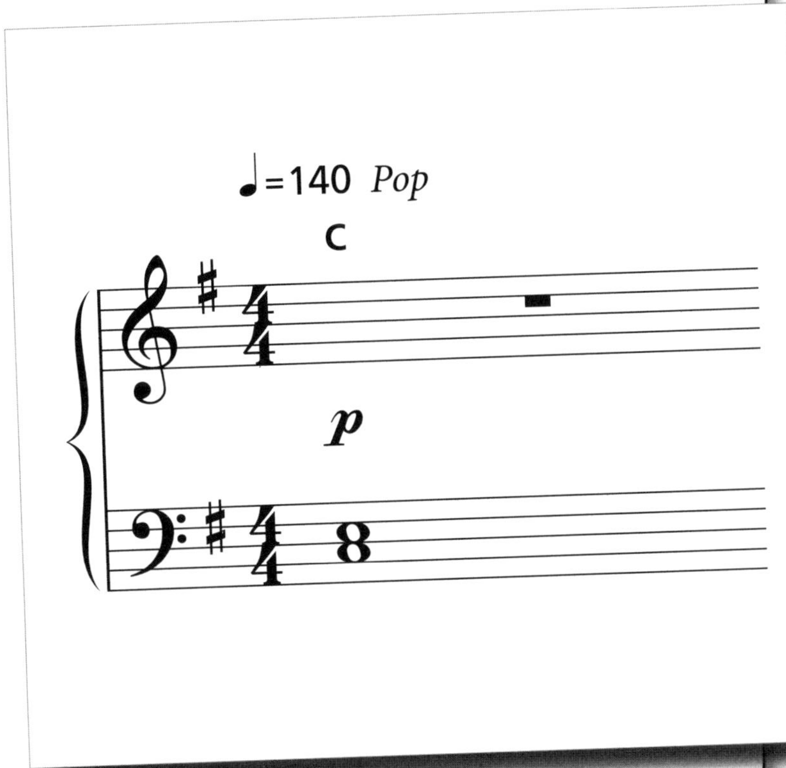

'Wildest Dreams' was a chart hit for American singer songwriter Taylor Swift and was the 5th single to be released from her popular album *1989.* The song was written by Taylor Swift, Max Martin and Johan Schuster (professionally known as Shellback), a common collaborative for Swift, with hits including three tracks on her earlier album *Red.* Together the trio created what has been described as a "dream pop power ballad" and although the song did well commercially it did receive some mixed reviews. Many felt that the sound was simply too comparable to that of Lana Del Rey, claiming that it was so similar that they couldn't tell whether the song was intended as a homage or a parody.

Nevertheless, the track went on to achieve success in the US charts where it peaked at a very respectable number 5. This gave Swift her 5th consecutive top ten single from her chart topping 3rd album, *1989.* The single was by no means her most successful in the UK, peaking at only number 40 on the UK Singles Chart. However, the album itself had great success in the UK and topped the chart on it's first week of release, thus becoming her second number one album in the UK.

Taylor Swift was born and raised in Pennsylvania but moved to Nashville at the young age of 14 in search of a music career. She originated as a country singer and honed the sounds of her then home Nashville. Swift quickly found success and was signed by Big Machine Records, making her the youngest person ever to have been signed by the Sony/ATV Music publishing house. In 2006 she released her self-titled debut album, which peaked at number 5 on the US album chart and included the track 'Our Song' – for this particular song she became the youngest ever artist to solely write and perform a number one hit for the Hot Country Songs chart.

In 2008 the crossover from country to pop began for Swift with her second album, *Fearless.* The album received rave reviews and became the highest selling US album of 2009. The album also won Swift a cool four Grammy awards, amongst which was the Album of the Year award for which she become the youngest ever winner.

Taylor Swift's repertoire has now reached an impressive six studio albums, a feat only achieved due to launching her career at such a young age. During her career she has received an impressive number of awards, including an outstanding total of 10 Grammy's (31 nominations). 'Wildest Dreams' became Swift's 13th top ten hit in the US, a clear representation of her success in the industry.

Wildest Dreams

Taylor Swift

B
G D Am C
f
[25]
G D Am C
[29]
G D Am
[33]
G D Am C
[37]
Em D
p
[41]
C Em D
[45]

Notes

The successful performance of this song depends on holding a steady tempo. Students should be encouraged to keep thinking in a strict quarter-note pulse throughout the opening eight measures in preparation for the introduction of the melody towards the end of measure 8.

Be aware of the different roles for each hand and ensure that the left-hand part steps back to allow the right-hand melody to shine through without the need to increase volume.

As the right-hand part follows the original vocal melody line, keep in mind that the rests are where the vocalist would breathe and allow this to guide you in shaping the musical phrases.

The right-hand part contains some interesting and varied syncopated patterns. Take time to play this through slowly to ensure that you are aware of exactly where the patterns repeat and differ and where the notes fall on or off beat. Counting out loud during practice sessions can be helpful. It is also worth spending time playing the right-hand part separately and securing the rhythmic patterns first before putting both hands together.

Let It Be

SONG TITLE: 'LET IT BE'
ALBUM: LET IT BE
RELEASED: 1970
LABEL: APPLE
GENRE: ROCK/POP/GOSPEL
WRITTEN BY: JOHN LENNON/ PAUL MCCARTNEY
PRODUCED BY: GEORGE MARTIN
US CHART PEAK: 1

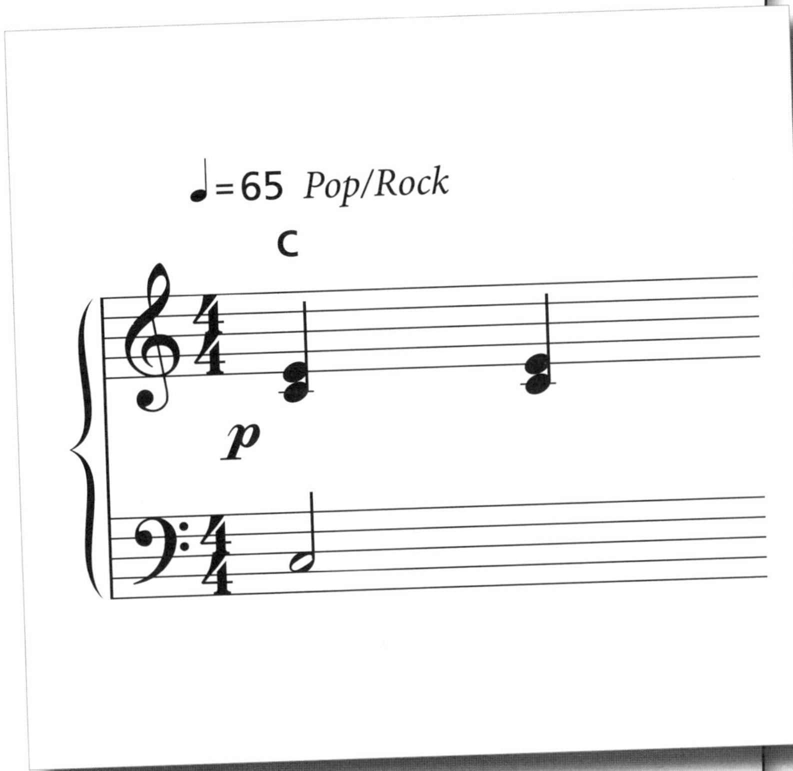

'Let it Be' was the final single to be released by The Beatles. Following an incredible career, this was the 22nd single to be released by the collective in only nine years. Shortly after writing the hit McCartney announced his soon to be departure from the band, a decision that would leave Beatlemania in disarray. The single was first released in March of 1970 and sadly the band announced their break up shortly afterwards in the April of that year.

'Let it Be' is taken from their 23rd studio album of the same name, although the album version of the track was in fact a little different to the single release. Slightly longer and featuring a second guitar solo, the album version was remixed by none other than Phil Spectre and introduced a more prominent instrumentation. The studio album, *Let it Be,* was sadly the last to be released by the British super group but it would be followed by solo careers for all four of them.

The Beatles are listed as the world's highest selling artists of all time and it could be argued that this isn't surprising, with 23 studio album releases in only nine years. When they first formed The Beatles had a mission to release an album every 6 months and they certainly did not disappoint. In 1962 they took the world by storm with their debut single 'Love Me Do' and suddenly Beatlemania was born. The band were enormously influential to the music industry, both then and now, and are regarded as largely responsible for the shift from Rock and Roll to Brit Pop. The Beatles have been awarded an outstanding fifteen Ivor Novello awards and seven Grammys, not to mention having been collectively listed in *The Times* 'The Twentieth Century's 100 most influential People'. In 1988 the band were inducted into the Rock and Roll Hall of Fame, a status that it's unlikely anyone would argue.

'Let it Be' was often regarded as a religious song, with references to 'Mother Mary' being misconstrued as biblical. However, McCartney actually wrote the song about his mother, Mary, who had sadly died of cancer when he was only fourteen. During a difficult time with the band he tells of a dream in which his mother visits him to tell him to "let it be". Although this is often misunderstood McCartney is known for assuring his listeners that they should interpret the song in whichever way they feel.

The single peaked at number 2 on the UK Singles Chart and topped the US Billboard Hot 100, where it stayed for two weeks. The song gave The Beatles their seventh consecutive year of charting a number 1 hit in the US, sharing the all time record of that time with Elvis Presley.

Let It Be

The Beatles

Words & Music by John Lennon & Paul McCartney

B
Am Em/G F C
f
[13]
C G F C
[15]
Am Em/G F C
[17]
C G F C
[19]
C
C G Am F
p
[21]
C G F C
[23]
F C/E Dm C B♭ Am G F C
[25]

Notes

The first four measures of this song are a scene-setting introduction with a strong melodic identity. Observing the *piano* dynamic marking will help ensure the solemnity of this introduction.

In the A section, the verse is comprised of two near-identical four measure phrases. This section maintains the solemnity of the introduction. While continuing to play quietly, allow the right-hand part to sing out over the left hand accompaniment, staying *legato* throughout. The left hand part will benefit from being played slightly detached and a little bit quieter than the melody line.

In the B section, the chorus is more passionate, releasing the previous inward feeling into an outward hopeful prayer. Pay attention to the *forte* dynamic here.

The fingering of the melody in measure 14 will need slow and careful practise, with the right hand alone.

The C section returns to the calm mood of the A section. The solemn mood in the first part of the song needs to be recreated, so it is important to observe the *piano* dynamic marking. Fingering in measures 25 and 26 will need to be practised slowly – hands separately at first, then together.

Be aware that there is B♭ in measure 25, which is then cancelled out in measure 26. Finally, make sure that the tied C major chord in measure 26 across to measure 27 is held for the full six beats.

I'm Not the Only One

SONG TITLE: 'I'M NOT THE ONLY ONE'
ALBUM: IN THE LONELY HOUR
RELEASED: 2014
LABEL: CAPITOL
GENRE: SOUL
WRITTEN BY: SAM SMITH/JAMES NAPIER
PRODUCED BY: JAMES NAPIER/ STEVE FITZMAURICE
US CHART PEAK: 5

'I'm Not the Only One' was the third single to be released from British singer songwriter Sam Smith's debut album, *In the Lonely Hour* (2014), preceded by 'Money on My Mind' and 'Stay with Me'. The song was written by Sam Smith and James Napier (better known in the industry as Jimmy Napes) and became a global hit for the pair, peaking at number 1 in the UK, number 5 in the US and achieving top ten positions in more than ten other countries worldwide.

The song itself was originally built around a piano ballad, but on production it became instrumentally impressive with escalating strings and gospel vocals. Smith himself felt that there were far more obvious tracks on *In the Lonely Hour* which could have been released but that 'I'm Not the Only One' showed a different and more sophisticated side to his debut album, an opinion which many reviewers shared. The track was met with praise and was described by many as a turning point on the album, showing real depth, impressive vocal skills and a spellbinding strings section.

Sam Smith first found success with his collaboration on Disclosure's single 'Latch', which peaked at number 11 on the UK Singles Chart in 2012. This was followed shortly by featured vocals on Naughty Boy's 'La La La' in 2013 which topped the charts on release and gave the singer his first taste for the top spot. In 2014 he released his debut album *In the Lonely Hour*, which despite initially receiving lukewarm reviews achieved global success – topping the album charts in 6 countries and becoming the UK's second-best selling album of 2014. Although his vocal was well received by reviewers the songwriting on the album was initially met with disappointment. However, on release of the 3rd single 'I'm Not the Only One' several of these opinions were quashed with many reviewers feeling that the song showed a richer complexity to Smith's songwriting.

In 2015 Smith and Napes achieved huge success with their song 'Writing's on the Wall' which they wrote together for the 24th James Bond film *Spectre.* The song won Smith both a Golden Globe and Academy Award for Best Original Song. The singer's second studio album, *'The Thrill Of It All'*, was released in 2017 and continued his success in the charts worldwide, topping both the UK and US album charts. Among his many achievements are 4 Grammy Awards, 3 Brit Awards, 7 UK number 1 singles and 4 People's Choice nominations.

I'm Not the Only One

Sam Smith

Words & Music by James Napier & Sam Smith

B♭maj7
F
C7
F
[14]
B
F
A
Dm
B♭maj7
F
A
Dm
mf
[17]
B♭maj7
F
A
Dm
B♭maj7
[20]
F
C7
F
[23]
F
C7
F
[26]

Notes

This soulful ballad has some challenging syncopations to negotiate in both hands. To ensure correct rhythmic patterns, students should keep thinking in a steady quarter-note pulse throughout. It will be helpful to mentally count a couple of measures to secure the tempo before starting to play.

If students find these syncopated phrases difficult, they should play them slowly without the ties. Once this can be done securely, the ties can be put back in.

While many of the syncopated patterns are identical in both hands (for example beats 3 and 4 of measure 1), pay careful attention to the occasions where hands are syncopated but move independently. A good example of this can be found in measures 9 and 10. These two measures would benefit from playing in isolation and at a much slower tempo to identify and learn how the parts fit together.

Technical Exercises

In this section you will be required to play a selection of exercises drawn from each of the groups below. The assessor will be looking for the speed of your response and will also give credit for the level of your musicality. Please see the syllabus guide for details on the marking criteria.

All scales and arpeggios need to be played hands separately, in straight feel, ascending and descending, in the keys, octaves and tempos shown. Pentatonic scales are right hand only. You may use your book for Group A and Group B. Group C exercises must be played from memory.

Note that Groups A and B need to be played to a click and any fingerings shown are suggestions only.

Group A: Scales
The tempo for this group is ♩= 60 bpm.

1. F major scale | right hand

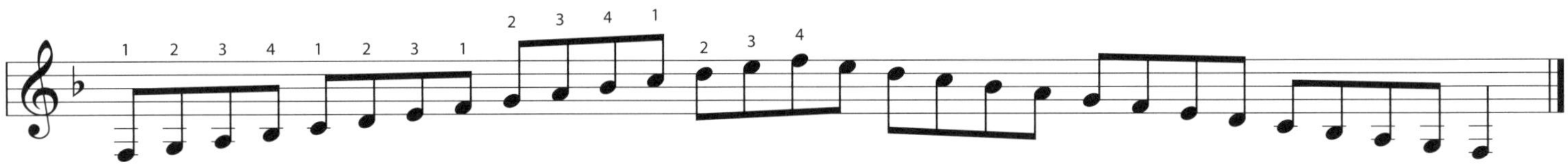

2. F major scale | left hand

3. G major scale | right hand

4. G major scale | left hand

5. D natural minor scale | right hand

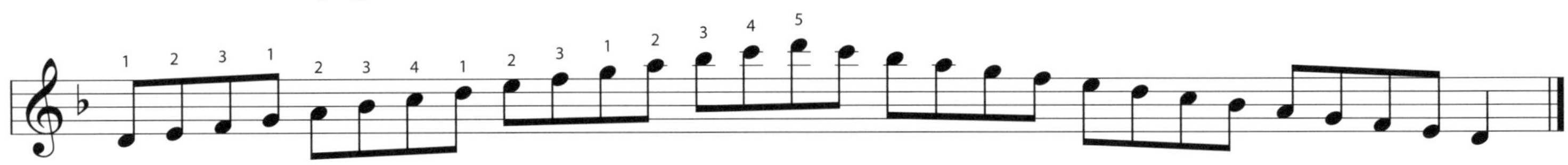

6. D natural minor scale | left hand

7. E natural minor scale | right hand

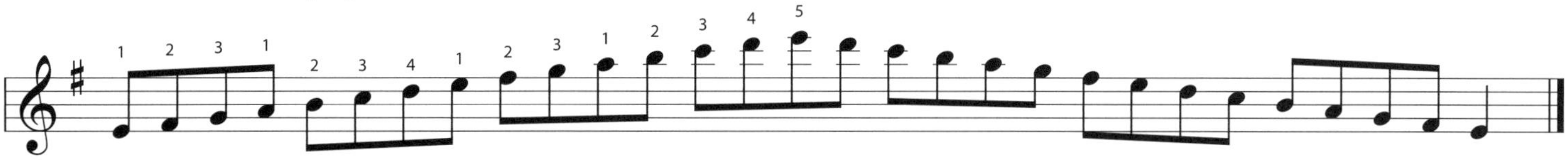

8. E natural minor scale | left hand

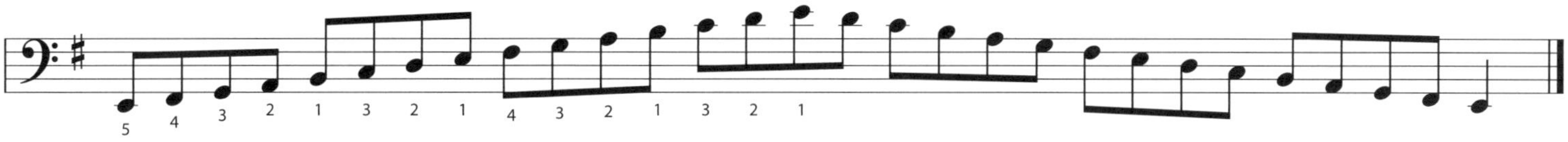

9. F major pentatonic scale | right hand

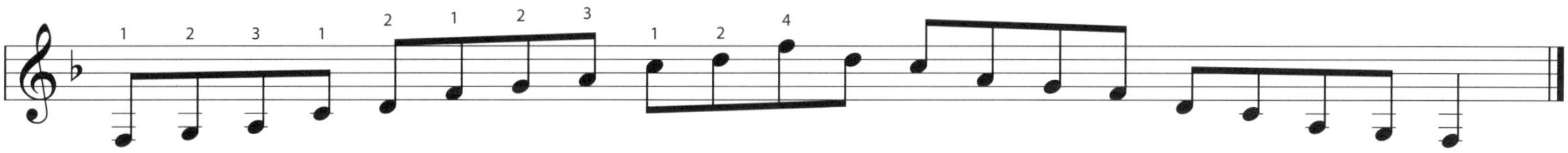

10. G major pentatonic scale | right hand

11. D minor pentatonic scale | right hand

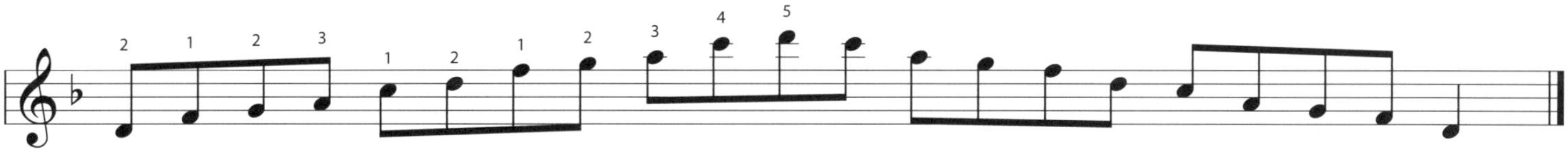

12. E minor pentatonic scale | right hand

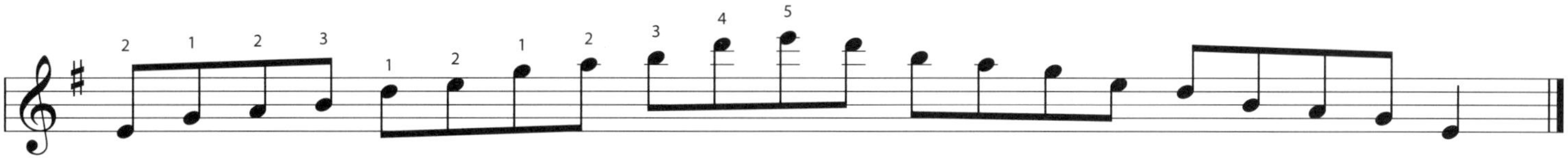

Group B: Arpeggios

The tempo for this group is ♩=100 bpm.

1. F major broken chord | right hand

2. F major broken chord | left hand

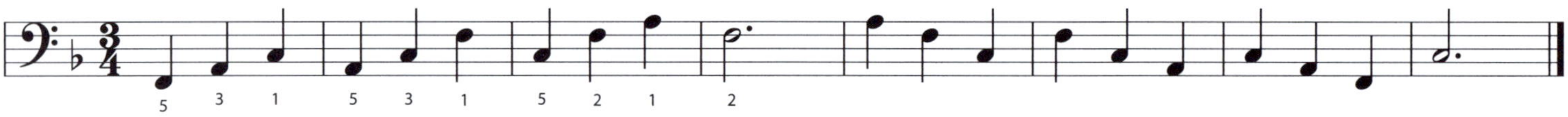

3. G major broken chord | right hand

4. G major broken chord | left hand

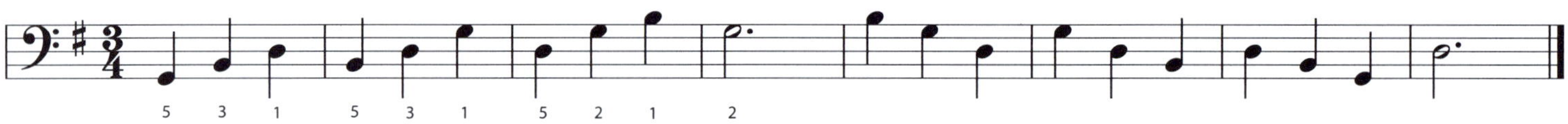

5. D natural minor broken chord | right hand

6. D natural minor broken chord | left hand

7. E natural minor broken chord | right hand

8. E natural minor broken chord | left hand

9. C diminished arpeggio | right hand

10. C diminished arpeggio | left hand

11. C augmented arpeggio | right hand

12. C augmented arpeggio | left hand

Group C: Chord Voicing

Diminished and Augmented triads

In the assessment you will be asked to play *either* the C diminished *or* the C augmented triads below, from memory. The assessor will state the exercise. This test is performed in free time (without backing track or click), but the assessor will be looking for the speed of your response.

1. C diminished

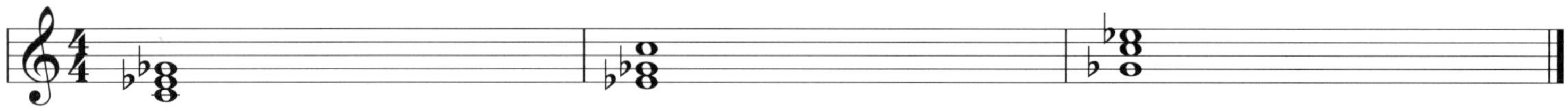

2. C augmented

Sight Reading

In the assessment, you have a choice between either a Sight Reading test or an Improvisation & Interpretation test. The assessor will ask you which one you wish to choose before commencing. Once you have decided you cannot change your mind.

In the sight reading test, the assessor will give you a 4–6 measure melody in the key of either G major or F major. You will first be given 90 seconds to practise, after which the assessor will play the backing track twice. The first time is for you to practise and the second time is for you to perform the final version for the assessment. For each playthrough, the backing track will begin with a one measure count-in. The tempo is ♩=70.

During the practice time, you will be given the choice of a metronome click throughout or a one measure count in at the beginning.

The backing track is continuous, so once the first playthrough has finished, the count in of the second playing will start immediately.

Sight Reading | Example 1

Sight Reading | Example 2

Please note: The tests shown are examples: The assessor will give you a different version in the assessment.

Improvisation & Interpretation

In the assessment, you have a choice between either a Sight Reading test or an Improvisation & Interpretation test. The assessor will ask you which one you wish to choose before commencing. Once you have decided you cannot change your mind.

In the Improvisation & Interpretation test, the assessor will give you a 4–6 measure chord progression in the key of either G major or F major. You will first be given 90 seconds to practise, after which the assessor will play the backing track twice. The first time is for you to practise and the second time is for you to perform the final version for the assessment. For each playthrough, the backing track will begin with a one measure count-in. The tempo is ♩= 70.

During the practice time, you will be given the choice of a metronome click throughout or a one measure count-in at the beginning.

The backing track is continuous, so once the first playthrough has finished, the count-in of the second playing will start immediately.

You are only required to improvise single note melodies, with either right or left hand. It is permissible to play chord voicings, but please note you will only be marked on melodic content.

Improvisation & Interpretation | Example 1

Improvisation & Interpretation | Example 2

Please note: The tests shown are examples: The assessor will give you a different version in the assessment

Ear Tests

In this section, there are two ear tests:

- Melodic Recall
- Chord Recognition

You will find one example of each type of test printed below and you will need to perform both of them in the assessment.

Test 1: Melodic Recall

The assessor will play you three consecutive notes. You will need to identify whether the last two notes are higher or lower than the first. This means you will need to tell the assessor whether the second note is higher or lower than the first, and whether the third note is higher or lower than the second. You will hear the test twice, each time with a one measure count-in. The tempo is ♩= 95 bpm.

For this exercise, please use the words 'higher' and 'lower' in your answer.

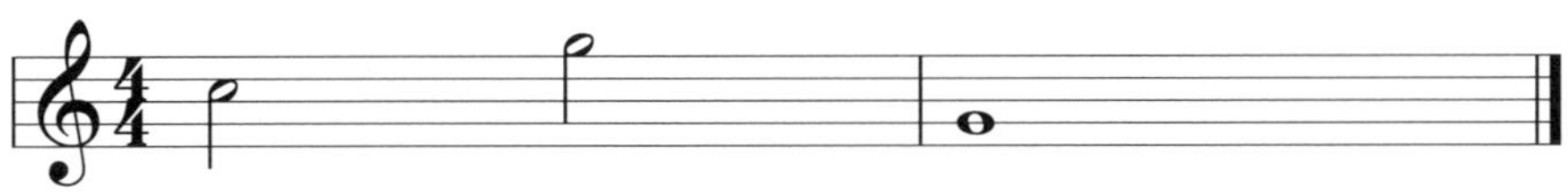

Please note: The test shown is an example. The assessor will give you a different version in the assessment.

Test 2: Chord Recognition

The assessor will play you a sequence of chords, each with a C root note. You will hear the chord sequence twice, each time with a one measure count-in. You will then be asked to identify the chord quality of each chord, from a choice of major, minor, diminished and augmented. The tempo is ♩= 95 bpm.

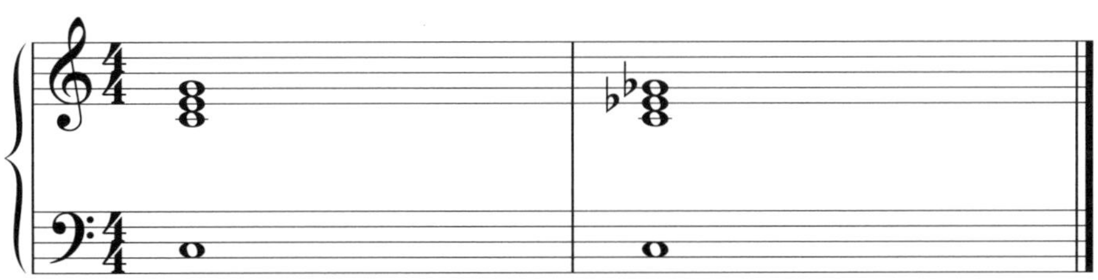

Please note: The test shown is an example. The assessor will give you a different version in the assessment.

General Musicianship Questions

The final part of your assessment is the General Musicianship Questions section, which features five questions relating to one of your choice of the performance pieces.

1. You will be asked a question relating to the harmony from a section of one of your pieces
2. You will be asked a question relating to the melody in a section of one of your pieces
3. You will be asked a question relating to the rhythms used in a section of one of your pieces
4. You will be asked a question relating to the technical requirements of one of your pieces
5. You will be asked a question relating to the genre of one of your pieces

Further guidance on the types of questions asked at this level/grade can be found at the RSL website *www.rslawards.com*

Entering Rockschool Assessments

Entering a Rockschool assessment is easy, just go online and follow our simple six step process. All details for entering online, dates, fees, regulations and Free Choice pieces can be found at *www.rslawards.com*

- All candidates should ensure they bring their own Level/Grade syllabus book to the assessment or have proof of digital purchase ready to show the assessor.

- All Level/Grade 6–8 candidates must ensure that they bring valid photo ID to their assessment.

Marking Schemes

DEBUT TO LEVEL/GRADE 8

ELEMENT	PASS	MERIT	DISTINCTION
Performance Piece 1	12–14 out of 20	15–17 out of 20	18+ out of 20
Performance Piece 2	12–14 out of 20	15–17 out of 20	18+ out of 20
Performance Piece 3	12–14 out of 20	15–17 out of 20	18+ out of 20
Technical Exercises	9–10 out of 15	11–12 out of 15	13+ out of 15
Sight Reading *or* Improvisation & Interpretation	6 out of 10	7–8 out of 10	9+ out of 10
Ear Tests	6 out of 10	7–8 out of 10	9+ out of 10
General Musicianship Questions	3 out of 5	4 out of 5	5 out of 5
TOTAL MARKS	60%+	74%+	90%+

PERFORMANCE CERTIFICATES | DEBUT TO LEVEL/GRADE 8

ELEMENT	PASS	MERIT	DISTINCTION
Performance Piece 1	12–14 out of 20	15–17 out of 20	18+ out of 20
Performance Piece 2	12–14 out of 20	15–17 out of 20	18+ out of 20
Performance Piece 3	12–14 out of 20	15–17 out of 20	18+ out of 20
Performance Piece 4	12–14 out of 20	15–17 out of 20	18+ out of 20
Performance Piece 5	12–14 out of 20	15–17 out of 20	18+ out of 20
TOTAL MARKS	60%+	75%+	90%+

Copyright Information

Tattooed Heart
(Edmonds/Dixon/Squire/Grande/Foreman/Thomas/Riddick Tynes)
Universal Music Publishing Limited/Kobalt Music Publishing Limited/Sony/ATV Music Publishing (UK) Limited/EMI Music Publishing Limited /Universal/MCA Music Limited

Hallelujah
(Cohen)
Sony/ATV Music Publishing (UK) Limited

Can You Feel The Love Tonight (from "The Lion King")
(John/Rice)
Universal Music Publishing Limited

Wildest Dreams
(Swift/Shellback/Martin)
Sony/ATV Music Publishing (UK) Limited/Kobalt Music Publishing Limited

Let It Be
(Lennon/McCartney)
Sony/ATV Music Publishing (UK) Limited

I'm Not The Only One
(Napier/Smith)
Downtown Music UK Limited/EMI Music Publishing Limited/Sony/ATV Music Publishing (UK) Limited

mcps

Piano Notation Explained

THE MUSICAL STAVE shows pitches and rhythms and is divided by lines into measures. Pitches are named after the first seven letters of the alphabet.

Grace Note: Play the grace note on or before the beat depending on the style of music, then move quickly to the note it leads onto.

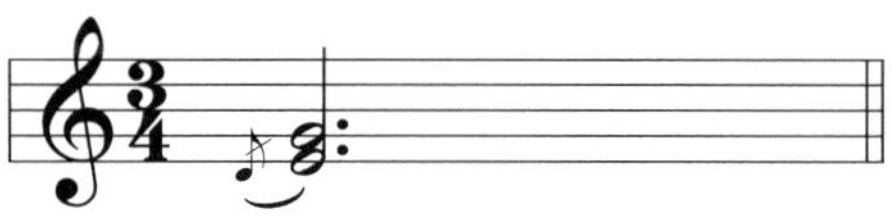

Pedal Marking: Depress and then release the sustain pedal. Multiple pedal operations in a short space of time may be simplified as shown in the last two beats of the measure below.

Spread Chord: Play the chord from the bottom note up (top down only if there is a downward arrow head). The final note should sound by the appropriate notated measure position.

Glissando: Play the notes between the notated pitches by sliding over the keyboard with the fingers or fingernails.

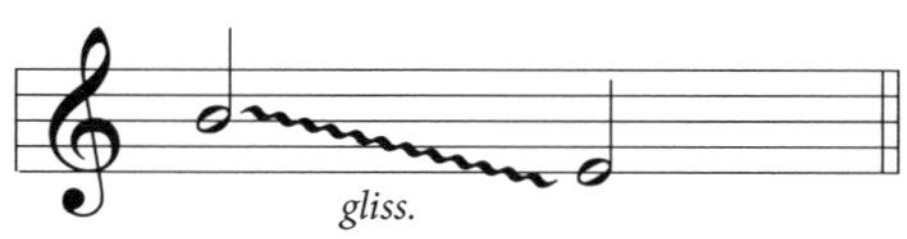

Tremolando: Oscillate at speed between marked notes.

Finger Markings: These numbers represent your fingers. 1 is the thumb, 2 the index finger and so on.

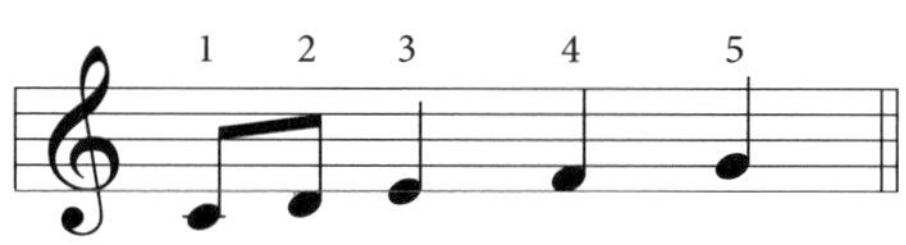

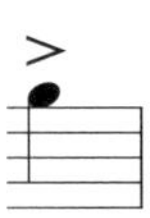 (accent) • Accentuate note (play it louder).

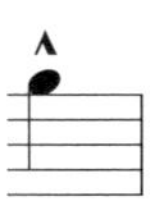 (accent) • Accentuate note with great intensity.

 (staccato) • Shorten time value of note.

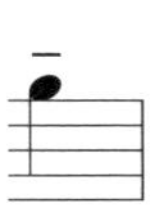 (accent) • Accentuate note with more arm weight.

D.𝄋. al Coda • Go back to the sign (𝄋), then play until the measure marked ***To Coda*** 𝄌 then skip to the section marked 𝄌 ***Coda.***

D.C. al Fine • Go back to the beginning of the song and play until the measure marked ***Fine*** (end).

Una Corda • Use soft pedal

 • Repeat the measures between the repeat signs.

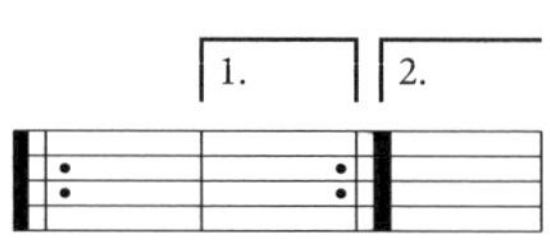

• When a repeated section has different endings, play the first ending only the first time and the second ending only the second time.